TO

FROM

OCCASION

THE

Christmas

CODE

DAILY DEVOTIONS
CELEBRATING
THE ADVENT SEASON

O. S. Hawkins

COUNTRYMAN®

A Division of Thomas Nelson Publishers

THOMAS NELSON
Since 1798

INTRODUCTION

For centuries Christians all over the world have celebrated the Advent season leading up to Christmas. *Advent* means "arrival, appearing, coming" and anticipates the coming of Christ to Bethlehem's stable. In the midst of all the busyness of this season, the celebrations, the shopping, the lights, the decorations, the parties, and all the other tinsel, trappings, and trimmings, Advent offers a time of spiritual preparation. It provides a time of reflecting on the true joy, peace, hope, and love that the coming of the Christ child makes possible for each and every one of us.

The Christmas Code embodies a devotional journey throughout the days of December up until Christmas Day. Each reading includes a scripture verse, a devotional thought, a Code Word, and a prayer. The Code Words serve to help unlock the blessings of each reading. Write them down; keep them with you to ponder throughout the day. And make the daily prayer a part of your own walk with Christ by repeating it often.

Use this little book as a time to look backward with earnest appreciation at Christ's first coming . . . and to look forward with eager anticipation to His Second Advent, His glorious appearing. Make the words to this centuries-old carol your own prayer this Christmas season:

> O come, O come, Emmanuel
> And ransom captive Israel
> That mourns in lowly exile here
> Until the Son of God appear.
> Rejoice! Rejoice! Emmanuel
> Shall come to thee, O Israel.

ROOTS: A CHRISTMAS GIFT

The book of the genealogy of Jesus Christ . . . And Jacob begot Joseph the husband of Mary, of whom was born Jesus who is called Christ.

MATTHEW 1:1, 16

There is no one like you. You are unique. No one has a fingerprint like yours, a DNA that exactly matches yours. Roots are important, and not just to plants. Your DNA shows what proclivities you may have regarding disease, intellect, temperament, and so much more.

There are forty-seven names listed in Matthew 1, most unpronounceable. Some are great, some not so great. From paupers to princes, shepherds to slaves, kings to harlots, spanning twenty-one centuries of human experience, the list ends in a stable on a starlit night with one name that is above every other name: Jesus!

The family tree of our Lord does not end with His ancestors, because His descendants—you and I—have been born again into His forever family.

Code Word: ROOTS

Can you tell me the full name of your great-grandfather? Or anything about his life? Chances are your own children's grandchildren will not even know your name. What really matters is this: are your true roots in Jesus' family tree?

....

Lord, may I be more concerned this season about being on Your list than on any other Christmas invitation list. In Jesus' name, amen.

THERE IS GRIEF IN THE
FAMILY TREE OF JESUS

*Abraham begot Isaac. . . . David the king begot
Solomon by her who had been the wife of Uriah.*

MATTHEW 1:2, 6

Talk about heartbreak, sorrow, misery, and grief—all those things are woven through the fabric of our Lord's family tree. Can you feel their grief behind these words? The grief of Abraham leaving all he had known to go to a land where he had never been. The grief of letting go of his firstborn, Ishmael, whom he loved. And what about King David? He had a son who died in infancy because of David's own sin. His son Absalom killed his brother Amnon, and if that were not enough to break a father's heart, Absalom led a revolt against his own dad.

But all these names in Christ's family tree don't hold a candle to grief this Christmas season. Jesus understands the grief in His ancestors and His descendants. Perhaps your own heart is heavy. Perhaps you have been misunderstood. Jesus was. He says, "I understand." Perhaps you are lonely. Jesus says, "I know the loneliness of Gethsemane's garden." He will bear your griefs and carry your sorrows . . . if you will let Him.

Code Word: GRIEF

The month of December holds more grief than any other. In the midst of all the tinsel and trappings, loneliness haunts so many. More suicides are attempted in this month than any other. Jesus understands your grief. Behind the lives of all these men and women in His family tree, we see grief, but they made it . . . and so can you.

Lord, thank You for bearing my grief and carrying my sorrows. I am leaning on You. In Jesus' name, amen.

THERE IS GRACE IN THE FAMILY TREE OF JESUS

Salmon begot Boaz by Rahab, Boaz begot Obed by Ruth.

MATTHEW 1:5

If time permitted, we could stop at each of the dozens of names in Christ's genealogy and speak of the grace behind their lives. But there are four obvious testimonies of grace that should catch our eyes. They are all women, and in that ancient world it was unheard-of to see women listed in genealogy tables.

First is Tamar (Matthew 1:3). Who was she? Let me introduce her. She once dressed as a prostitute, seduced her father-in-law, and had an illegitimate child (Genesis 38). We also read of Rahab (Matthew 1:5). She was the town prostitute of ancient Jericho. Next comes Ruth (v. 5). She was a member of a race that began in incest and worshipped pagan gods. Finally we meet Bathsheba (v. 6). She lived in adultery with King David.

How did these women find their way into Jesus' own family tree? Only one word: grace! God's unmerited favor.

Code Word: FAVOR

There is good news this Christmas. Where sin abounds, grace much more abounds . . . for you. What is the Lord telling us? I don't think He is speaking softly—"If anyone is in Christ, he is a new creation; old things have passed away; behold, all things have become new" (2 Corinthians 5:17).

Lord, thank You for giving me what I never deserved . . . an amazing gift: grace! In Jesus' name, amen.

THERE IS GOD IN THE
FAMILY TREE OF JESUS

And Jacob begot Joseph the husband of Mary, of
whom was born Jesus who is called Christ.

MATTHEW 1:16

Note carefully what today's verse says . . . and doesn't say. It does not say, "Joseph begot Jesus." Here the repetition of the "begots" ends. The "whom" in Greek is feminine singular, referring only to Mary and not to Joseph. Can you see God the Father right here in the family tree of Jesus? Jesus was the virgin-born son of Mary, in whose womb the Father implanted His Son. Hundreds of years earlier, the prophet Isaiah had said the virgin birth would be the "sign" of the long-awaited Messiah (Isaiah 7:14).

It is because Jesus was Mary's seed (the seed of a woman, Genesis 3:15) and not the seed of Joseph that entitles Him to be your Savior and Lord. The virgin birth is the bedrock of His authority.

Some see only grief. But look closer and you will find grace. And, if you look close enough, you will see the hand of God molding, making, forming, and fashioning you. He has been there all along.

CODE WORD: BOOK

The only book that ultimately matters is the Lamb's Book of Life, where the names of all those who have put their trust in Christ are listed. Is your name in that book? Jesus said, "Do not rejoice . . . that the spirits are subject to you, but rather rejoice because your names are written in heaven" (Luke 10:20).

....

Lord, thank You that You are working in my life this very moment, forming and fashioning me into Your very image. In Jesus' name, amen.

UPON A MIDNIGHT CLEAR

She brought forth her firstborn Son . . . and laid Him in a manger.

LUKE 2:7

If you are like me, you type hundreds of words each day. Let me ask you a question. Are the keys you type on black, gray, or white? The truth is, most people cannot give a definitive answer without looking at the keys, even though they look at them several times every single day. The point? There are a lot of things in life we see but don't really see.

Take the nativity scene. You have seen it depicted thousands of times, but have you really *see* it? I love the feature on my mobile phone that allows me to crop my photos. Recently we took a family picture. Susie and I in the middle, with the grandkids and their parents flanking us. We have a common "enemy" with our grandkids—their parents! I cropped them out and have a beautiful photo of Susie, me, and the grandkids!

Let's crop the nativity. Look at the entire nativity scene. It is a worship service. Crop it a bit and you find a family in the middle: Joseph, Mary, and the Christ. Crop it more and in the center you see Jesus only.

Code Word: CROP

Take a picture of the nativity set in your
home. Crop out everything but Jesus.
Christmas is about Jesus. Keep Him in the
middle of your Christmas this year.

....

Lord, in the midst of all the hustle and
bustle of this season, help me focus on
You. In Jesus' name, amen.

LOOK AT THE BIG PICTURE—
IT'S A WORSHIP SERVICE

*"Glory to God in the highest, and on earth peace,
goodwill toward men!"*

LUKE 2:14

Look at the nativity, and you see a worship service. Angels hover over it like drones. Common, smelly shepherds and sophisticated wise men bow down. Worship flows from everyone toward the child.

It is difficult to imagine any greater contrasts than what we see at the nativity. They were different socially. Shepherds were low on the socioeconomic level. Wise men were so socially acceptable they entered the king's palace. They were different educationally. Shepherds had no formal education, while the wise men were famed for knowledge. God is telling us that no matter who you are or where you are from, any and all can come to Christ and worship Him.

Christmas, first and foremost, is about worship. Those at the manger were not there simply admiring this Child. They were worshipping Him. Make sure worship is first on your Christmas list.

Code Word: MANGER

Think about it: "She . . . laid Him in a manger," a feeding trough for the animals (Luke 2:7). Had He been born in a palace, only the elite would have access. But any and all can approach a manger. Jesus is still accessible to you and anyone who will join the shepherds in bowing before Him.

. . . .

Lord, help me keep the worship of You in the heart of my Christmas this year. Glory to God in the highest. In Jesus' name, amen.

CROP THE NATIVITY, AND IN THE MIDDLE YOU WILL FIND A FAMILY

So it was, that while they were there, the days were completed for her to be delivered.

LUKE 2:6

Look in the middle of the nativity and you find a little family. Christmas is about family. God entrusted His own Son to a human family, just like yours. He could have circumvented the family, but He didn't. God put His own stamp of approval on the family.

Family is important to God. Think about it. He instituted the family long before He did the church. He placed His own Son in a family with relationships and domestic responsibilities. So Jesus was raised in Nazareth in a family unit.

Later, while hanging on the cross, He spotted Mary and instructed John to care for her. Jesus was a family man. His was a blended family, when you think about it. Family is precious to Him.

The nativity has a family in the middle of it for good reason. God is pro-family. Christmas has its own unique way of drawing families together.

CODE WORD: FAMILY

Where do we most want to be at Christmas? Home. We drive long distances to sleep on couches and floors to be home for Christmas. Make sure you hold your family close to your heart, and don't be hesitant to say, "I love you."

....

Lord, thank You for family, and help me do my part in drawing my family closer this Christmas. In Jesus' name, amen.

P THE NATIVITY MORE, ND IN THE CENTER YOU WILL FIND A SAVIOR

"There is born to you this day in the city of David a Savior, who is Christ the Lord."

LUKE 2:11

I love Rembrandt's portrayal of the nativity. One great beam of light falls upon the baby Jesus so that all the other participants are somewhat shrouded in shadow. He wanted nothing to take away from the significance of Christ.

Christmas is really about Christ. And, primarily, Christ alone. Not only is He the center of the nativity scene, He is the center of all of human history. His birth divided all of human history into "before" and "after" Christ. And, if you don't believe this, just think about it at the end of this month when you change your calendar. His birth points the way for all men and women to see that the road to our eternal home is through Him.

If the nativity were your own life, who or what would be in the center? He longs to be the center of your life this holiday season.

Code Word: TRANSPORT

If you could transport yourself back in time to that stable, would you see yourself standing somewhere off to the side, observing? Or would you find yourself on your knees, joining the angelic choir saying, "Glory to God in the highest!"?

....

Lord, my desire is to be a worshipper. And You alone are worthy of my worship. In Jesus' name, amen.

LET US GO TO BETHLEHEM

"Let us now go to Bethlehem and see this thing that has come to pass, which the Lord has made known to us."

LUKE 2:15

It was a dark night . . . yet there was light! The Light of the world had come. Bethlehem almost missed it. No room. So the young, pregnant Jewish girl found herself without the decency of even a clean sheet or a simple cot. In her hour of labor, her bed was straw in a stable. And, when the babe was born, she herself, with trembling fingers, wrapped Him in cloths and laid Him in the feeding trough.

Down the hillside a group of shepherds had a surprise visit from heaven. They rushed to the stable, found the babe, and returned "glorifying and praising God" (Luke 2:20).

Let's become Bethlehem ourselves. We find in this little village a place of potential, providence, and privilege. The Lord longs for you to become a Bethlehem in your own right. That is, to awaken to the fact that you are a person of potential, providence, and privilege.

CODE WORD: SURPRISE

Can you imagine the surprise of the shepherds that night when heaven burst open before them and the angelic chorus in perfect harmony declared the Lord's birth? This is usually the way it happens . . . surprised by God. Be prepared for Him to meet you in a surprising way this Christmas.

....

Lord, help me live in anticipation of a heavenly surprise this day. In Jesus' name, amen.

BETHLEHEM IS A PLACE OF POTENTIAL

> *"But you, Bethlehem . . . though you are little among the thousands of Judah, yet out of you shall come forth . . . the One . . . whose goings forth are from of old, from everlasting."*
>
> MICAH 5:2

Think of it. Of all the places for the Messiah to be born, God chose Bethlehem. One would have thought it might be in a much more prominent place, like Jerusalem. Bethlehem reminds us that in God's economy the small shall become great, and the last shall be first. Bethlehem was a place of potential, and even though you may feel insignificant, like Bethlehem, so are you!

As the Lord looks at you, He doesn't see you for what you are, but for what you could become. This is the message of Bethlehem. God did not come to Caesar's palace to be born, nor to Herod's court. He arrived quietly, almost unannounced in a seemingly insignificant village.

God is reminding you today that in His eyes you have potential for greatness. See yourself as a Bethlehem. You, too, are a person of potential.

Code Word: PROSPECT

Your prospects are limitless. God sees you not for who you are, but for who you can become. When He first saw Peter, He said, "You are a small pebble but will become a great rock" (John 1:42, author's paraphrase). Peter believed it and later became the leader of the early church.

....

Lord, help me see today what You see—incredible potential in me. In Jesus' name, amen.

BETHLEHEM IS A PLACE OF PROVIDENCE

"But you, Bethlehem Ephrathah,
Though you are little among the thousands of Judah,
Yet out of you shall come forth to Me
The One to be Ruler in Israel,
Whose goings forth are from of old,
From everlasting."

MICAH 5:2

Long centuries before His birth, the prophets foretold that Christ would be born in Bethlehem. But how? Joseph and Mary resided seventy miles north, in Nazareth. God put the whole world in motion to fulfill His Word. A decree went out from Caesar Augustus that everyone was to go to the place of their family lineage to pay taxes. So Joseph, because he was in the line of David, left Nazareth with his very pregnant wife on a long journey of inconvenience.

Many of the things in our lives that on the surface appear inconvenient, may just be the hand of God's providence getting us to our own Bethlehem.

Bethlehem reminds us that what God promises, He performs—no matter what. Bethlehem is a place of providence, and so are you.

Code Word: PROVIDENCE

God is at work, behind the scenes in your life, right now: "The Most High rules in the kingdom of men" (Daniel 4:17). God has not abdicated His throne. He is at work in your life when you are not even aware.

....

Lord, what You have promised You will perform. Make me a Bethlehem today. In Jesus' name, amen.

BETHLEHEM IS A PLACE OF PRIVILEGE

*My little children, for whom I labor in birth again
until Christ is formed in you.*

GALATIANS 4:19

What an awesome privilege to be the handpicked city to cradle the Son of God. Why Bethlehem? Why not Jerusalem, the seat of religious power? Or Rome, the center of political power? Or Athens, the center of intellectual power? God was sending a message. The hope of our world is not in religion, politics, or philosophy. God privileged the little village of Bethlehem to send the message—the hope of the world is in a Savior!

This Christmas could become a Bethlehem moment for you. Like Bethlehem, you can awaken to a brand-new world. The same Christ born in Bethlehem can be born again in you. Paul puts it this way: "I labor in birth again until Christ is formed in you." If you think Bethlehem is privileged to be His birthplace, what a greater privilege for Christ to be born in you.

Thinking of Bethlehem, Phillips Brooks wrote, "The hopes and fears of all the years are met in thee tonight."

Code Word: EXPECTATION

One of the code words of Advent is
hope—that sense of expectation, the feeling
that something good is going to happen.
Bethlehem almost missed the moment.
But you can awaken to a brand-new
hope by allowing your life to become a
Bethlehem—the great privilege of having
Christ born again in you.

....

*Lord, thank You, not just for hope but
for the realization that You are truly
alive in me, in this moment. In Jesus'
name, amen.*

What's in a Name?

*"You shall call His name Jesus. . . . They shall call
His name Immanuel."*

MATTHEW 1:21, 23

There is an interesting psychology in the naming of
our children. Some are named with family names
to retain a family heritage. I am often asked what O. S.
stands for, and I am quick to say, "Omar Sharif." But
the truth is, my initials represent family names—Otis
Swafford. And now you know why I use O. S. on the
cover of this book. Others are named for an attribute
their parents desire their child to achieve in life: Faith
or Hope, for example.

In the Bible, names have specific meanings. Jesus
changed Simon's name to Peter because he saw
the potential for him to be a "rock." Joseph's name
was changed to Barnabas (which means "Son of
Encouragement") because every time he had center
stage, he was encouraging the early believers.

During these days let's pause to think of the names
given to our Lord. The mission of Christmas is in His
name: Jesus. And the message of Christmas is in His
name as well: Immanuel.

CODE WORD: NAME

What does your name mean? The next time you sign a check or a note and look at your name, think about it. Names matter . . . and the one name that is above all others is *Jesus*!

....

Lord, help me wear the name "Christian" with integrity and honor today. In Jesus' name, amen.

THE MISSION OF CHRISTMAS
IS IN A NAME—JESUS

"And she will bring forth a Son, and you shall call His name JESUS, for He will save His people from their sins."

MATTHEW 1:21

The name *Jesus* is a transliteration of the Hebrew name *Joshua*, which means "Jehovah saves." His very name, Jesus, tell us of the mission upon which He came from heaven to earth—to "save His people from their sins."

Jesus is our Lord's intensely personal name. Have you noticed how difficult it is for some people to say this name, Jesus? They find it much easier to refer to Him as God or Lord or Christ or "the man upstairs." But there is something about speaking the name Jesus. Say it now. Out loud. Jesus is His most personal name, and only those who truly know Him in the free pardoning of their sin find it easy to speak His name.

He came to save you from your sins. Open your heart to Him. He said, "I came to seek and to save those who were lost" (Luke 19:10, author's paraphrase).

CODE WORD: LOST

Say that word: *lost*. Say it again out loud. Without Christ that is what we are— lost beyond hope, lost beyond time, lost beyond eternity, lost, forever lost. But when we open our hearts to Him, we begin to know Him by His up-close and personal name: Jesus!

....

Jesus, thank You for coming on a mission for the express purpose of saving me. In Jesus' name, amen.

THE MESSAGE OF CHRISTMAS IS IN A NAME—IMMANUEL

And they shall call His name Immanuel, which is translated, "God with us."

MATTHEW 1:23

The name *Immanuel* is a translation of two Hebrew words expressing "God is with us." *God* with us. Not some prophet or teacher or holy man. But God Himself clothed in human flesh—*with us*! He came to where we are so we could go eternally to where He is. God . . . always with us.

God—that is majesty. With us—that is mercy. God—that is glory. With us—that is grace. He came to be with us, to give us what we never deserved and to not give us what we did deserve.

He could not be Jesus without being Immanuel. That is, in order to save us, He first had to come and be with us, taking on human flesh. At Bethlehem we see God with us. At Calvary we see God for us. At Pentecost we see God in us.

CODE WORD: WITH

It is one thing to be *for* someone but another thing to be *with* someone, to stand by his or her side in good times as well as bad, times of sorrow as well as times of joy. This is our Lord's name: Immanuel. He is with you right now. And when He left this earth, He did so with these final words: "Lo, I am with you always" (Matthew 28:20).

....

Lord, nowhere I go today will I be without You. You are with me always. In Jesus' name, amen.

SIGNPOSTS AT CHRISTMAS

"The Lord Himself will give you a sign: Behold, the virgin shall conceive and bear a Son, and shall call His name Immanuel."

ISAIAH 7:14

What is a sign? It is something that is intended to do two things: grab your attention and then tell you something. You may be driving on a hazardous mountain road and see a flashing sign warning you to slow down for a sharp curve ahead. Billboards are designed to grab your attention, to do it fast, and then to leave you with a message you won't soon forget.

The Bible tells us there is a "sign" regarding the promised coming Messiah. And this sign, designed to get our attention and tell us something, is that a "virgin shall conceive and bear a Son." This is humanly impossible. It would take a divine miracle.

Jesus was virgin-born. He was not God and man. He is the God-man, the "only begotten Son . . . of the Father" (John 1:18), who put His own seed in a young virgin girl.

Code Word: SIGN

Today, as you do your Christmas shopping and see a hundred signs grabbing your attention to tell you something, let each one be a reminder that the "sign" that Jesus is Lord is the virgin birth, the bedrock of your salvation.

....

Lord, if I could understand it all, there wouldn't be much to it. I believe . . . by faith. In Jesus' name, amen.

SHE LAID HIM IN A MANGER

She brought forth her firstborn Son . . . and laid Him in a manger.

LUKE 2:7

These words grab my heart more than any others: "She . . . laid Him in a manger." Not a nice little wooden cradle like we see in a manger scene. But a rock-hewn cattle trough in a cavelike stable where your sandals squashed in the dung as you walked and the nauseating smell of the animals filled your nostrils. She laid Him in a manger. Think of it. Sickness, disease, death were likely possibilities.

How desperately alone from family and friends Mary must have felt when she realized the babe would be born far away from home. In her hour of pain, her bed was straw in a stable, and when the baby was born, she herself, with trembling fingers "wrapped Him in swaddling cloths, and laid Him in a manger."

"No room" was not just the message of Bethlehem but the theme of Jesus' life. But those who find Him and make room in their hearts for Him understand the true message of Christmas.

Code Word: ACCESS

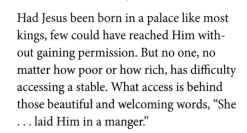

Had Jesus been born in a palace like most kings, few could have reached Him without gaining permission. But no one, no matter how poor or how rich, has difficulty accessing a stable. What access is behind those beautiful and welcoming words, "She . . . laid Him in a manger."

. . . .

Lord, thank You that anyone may come to You . . . and that includes me. In Jesus' name, amen.

MARY, DID YOU KNOW?

But Mary kept all these things and pondered them in her heart.

LUKE 2:19

Mary. A young girl playing in the streets of Nazareth with her friends one day and finding she is pregnant, though a virgin and unmarried, the next. Her initial response? "How can this be?" (Luke 1:34).

After Jesus was born, it all began to sink in, Mary "pondered" all these things in her heart. The word picture is of a cake, with all the ingredients in a bowl, being stirred up. She was putting it all together, stirring it up in her mind . . . the prophecies . . . the angel's message . . . the virgin birth.

She knew those chubby little hands would never be adorned with expensive gold or silver rings. They were destined for other things, like touching lepers, forming spittle for blind eyes, and eventually being pierced with Roman spikes. But she also knew that millions of us would follow in His steps. She "pondered" all these things and kept them to herself.

CODE WORD: BAKE

As you enjoy a host of Christmas pastries this holiday season, let each bite remind you of Mary pondering all those things in her heart. Get by yourself, contemplate it, mediate on it, and ponder the wonder of Bethlehem.

....

Lord, I honor You in pausing to give honor to the woman You chose to nurture Your own Son. Help me to be a ponderer this season. In Jesus' name, amen.

THE FORGOTTEN MAN AT THE MANGER

An angel . . . appeared to him . . . saying, "Joseph . . .
do not be afraid to take to you Mary your wife, for
that which is conceived in her is of the Holy Spirit."

MATTHEW 1:20

Joseph is the one person in the Christmas drama seldom mentioned and never quoted, yet the entire narrative hinges on his faithfulness. Mary is quoted. As are Elizabeth, Zacharias, the shepherds, the wise men, Herod, Simeon, and even the angels. But there is no record of anything Joseph ever said.

We hear a lot of carols at Christmastime. There are songs about Mary, the wise men, the shepherds, the angels, the star. Everyone has a carol about them, except Joseph. Hardly anyone sings of him at Christmas.

But there is a reason God chose Joseph to mentor and raise His own son. He was faithful. Each time God sent him a message through an angel, he obeyed immediately (Matthew 1:18–25; 2:13–15; 2:20–22). Our legacy from this forgotten man at the manger is not in what he said but in what he did. The entire story hinges on his obedience to God.

CODE WORD: ORDINARY

Maybe no one takes notes of what you say.
Perhaps you have never written a book.
Like me, you are just an ordinary person.
Learn a lesson from another one of us,
Joseph, a common carpenter. God uses
ordinary people. He chooses people like
you and me to do as He commands.

....

*Lord, help me see today that what I do
speaks louder than anything I might
say. In Jesus' name, amen.*

MAKING THE MOST OF CHRISTMAS

Then the shepherds returned, glorifying and praising
God for all the things that they had heard and seen,
as it was told them.

LUKE 2:20

How can you make the most of Christmas? For some it is all about decorating the house or tree, getting that special gift, seeing relatives, or getting invited to that certain someone's party. But making the most of Christmas is so much more than any of these things.

Join the shepherds this year in making these next few days a time of "glorifying and praising God," a time of celebrating all that Christmas is and means. God "inhabits the praises" of His people (Psalm 22:3 KJV). This is where and when God feels at home—in the midst of your praise.

Note the shepherds "returned." Where? To their homes and businesses. What an impact this must have had on those who knew them best. May God give you the grace to follow these shepherds and make the most of Christmas this year.

Code Word: JOY

Another of the code words of Advent is *joy*. Celebrate Christ above all other things this holiday season. Sing it—"Joy to the world, the Lord has come!"

....

Lord, thank You for the joy only You can give. Let's celebrate Your birth! In Jesus' name, amen.

MAKING EVEN MORE OF CHRISTMAS

*Now when they had seen Him, they made widely
known the saying which was told them concerning
this Child.*

LUKE 2:17

Don't just celebrate Christmas this year; circulate it!
The shepherds became verbal witnesses of what
they had seen and heard. They had seen God in human
flesh. Their own eyes had looked upon the One the
prophets had foretold for centuries. They heard the
music of heaven. And they could not help but speak to
others about what they had seen and heard.

God chose a bunch of simple shepherds to be the
first to circulate the good news of Christ's coming.
Others in Bethlehem were of more importance and
higher prominence. Surely their testimony would
have borne more weight. But God still has His ways of
confounding the wise.

Christmas is just another warm and fuzzy, sen-
timental story unless you circulate it. Christmas
provides a great opportunity to share the good news
with family and friends whose hearts will be more
open than at any other time of the year.

CODE WORD: TELL

Jesus tells us to "go and tell" (see Matthew 28:19–20). We seem to find it much easier and safer to change this to "come and hear." Ask God to give you the boldness of the shepherds this Christmas to make "widely known" the true message of Christmas.

. . . .

Lord, I want to deliver Your good news. And the headline reads, "Jesus saves." In Jesus' name, amen.

Backstage on Christmas Eve

"I have come . . . to do Your will."

HEBREWS 10:7

All over our world, churches large and small are presenting Christmas plays and pageants. What amazes me is how much goes on backstage before the curtain ever rises. There are props to be made, costumes to be sewn, music to be rehearsed, lines to be memorized, and so much more.

On this Christmas, with all the attention on Bethlehem and the manger, think for a minute about what was transpiring backstage . . . in heaven, that is. Our Lord was saying a farewell to His Father. Laying aside His glory, He stepped over the portals of heaven into a smelly Eastern stable.

And what would He say to the Father as He departed, when the curtain rose on the greatest event in human history? I go "to do Your will."

That for which we had been waiting and to which the prophets had been pointing was coming . . . and for the express purpose of doing the Father's will.

CODE WORD: BACKSTAGE

All of heaven was looking over those portals that starlit night in Bethlehem. The "fulness of the time" (Galatians 4:4 KJV) had come. Although most on earth were oblivious, those in heaven were watching and worshipping. Remember: what is onstage is not always the whole story.

. . . .

Lord, to think of what You left to come to give me life moves me to want "to do Your will." In Jesus' name, amen.

CHRISTMAS EVE IN HEAVEN—A WORD OF CONDESCENSION

When He came into the world, He said: . . . "a body You have prepared for Me."

HEBREWS 10:5

What a step—from the splendor of heaven to the womb of a woman and finally to a stable in Bethlehem. There is so much behind those words "a body You have prepared for Me." God is Spirit, and yet He stepped into a body of flesh to identify with you and, ultimately, to be your own sin-bearer.

This is condescension of the first and finest order. God became as helpless as a tiny seed planted in the womb of a young virgin girl. Then, as helpless as a baby totally dependent on someone else's care.

Look at Mary. To paraphrase the master wordsmith Max Lucado, she is in labor . . . her back is aching . . . her feet are swollen . . . she is sweating profusely . . . and having rapid contractions. The baby's head appears as she groans and pushes Him into the world. And He arrives! God in flesh has come to visit us: "A body You have prepared for Me."

CODE WORD: BODY

Pinch yourself. Flesh, that is what God became . . . for you. So that He might say, "I understand." He came down to take a physical body so that one day you could go up and have a spiritual body. He came to be with you so that you could one day go to be with Him.

....

Lord, there is nothing I go through that You don't understand. In Jesus' name, amen.

CHRISTMAS EVE IN HEAVEN—A WORD OF COMPREHENSION

When He came into the world, He said: . . . "I have come . . . to do Your will."

HEBREWS 10:5–7

Jesus not only comprehended the Father's will; He came to perform it. This is the primary purpose of His Advent, to do the Father's will. He commenced this theme here on Christmas Eve and concluded with it thirty-three years later in Gethsemane's garden: "Not My will, but Yours, be done" (Luke 22:42).

There are two very important one-syllable, two-letter words in our scripture for the day: "I have come *to do* Your will." The Lord didn't come to find the will of the Father but "to do" His will. His journey to Golgotha was not primarily to save us, but to be obedient to His Father's will.

Should we do less this Christmas season? True success in your life comes not in knowing the will of God, but in doing it.

Code Word: PEACE

Peace is one of the most beautiful attributes of Advent. And doing the Father's will is what brings true peace to this special night. No wonder we call Him the "Prince of Peace" (Isaiah 9:6).

....

Lord, put Your peace on me now, the peace You give that the world cannot take away. In Jesus' name, amen.

CHRISTMAS DAY

Thanks be to God for His indescribable gift!
2 CORINTHIANS 9:15

It's the Christmas miracle: "The Word became flesh and dwelt among us" (John 1:14).

Jesus was the unique God-man. As God, He walked on water, calmed the storm, healed the sick, and rose from the dead. As man, He got thirsty and tired; He felt sorrow and pain.

Jesus came to earth as a helpless, tiny seed planted in the womb of a young Jewish virgin. Forty weeks later, Jesus was born in a filthy stable.

Jesus was born in Bethlehem. Its name meaning "the house of bread," Bethlehem was the birthplace of the Bread of Life. God wanted people to know that the hope of the world is a Savior.

On this Christmas Day, in the midst of family and friends, gadgets and gifts, join Paul in exclaiming, "Thanks be to God for His indescribable gift!" (2 Corinthians 9:15).

CODE WORD: LOVE

The very definition of our Lord is this: "God is love" (1 John 4:8). This Advent season comes to a close with this word: *love*. Love is the oxygen of the kingdom. Without it there is no Christmas. "For God so loved the world that He gave His only begotten Son" (John 3:16). Believe on Him.

. . . .

Lord, I love You on this Christmas Day because You first loved me. Happy birthday, Jesus. In Jesus' name, amen.

GOD'S PERSONAL CHRISTMAS GIFT TO YOU

Christmas is a time for giving gifts . . . and receiving gifts. Think about that Christmas gift you received. What did you do to get it? You didn't earn it. You didn't necessarily deserve it. All you had to do on Christmas morning to make it yours was to unwrap it and receive it. After all, it was freely given by someone who loves you.

The Bible says, "The gift of God is eternal life through Jesus Christ our Lord" (Romans 6:23 KJV). Heaven! It can't be earned. It can't be bought. It, too, is undeserved. It is God's gift to you from Someone who loves you very much. And all you have to do to make it your own is receive it . . . by faith.

The message of Christ is not confined to December and does not end in the cradle. It continues to the cross, where Christ took your sin in His own body and paid your sin debt in full. He was buried and rose again on the third day. But this is not all. After the cradle and the cross comes the crown. He is coming back, no longer as a suffering servant, but as the King of all kings and the Lord of all lords.

After journeying through *The Christmas Code*, perhaps you feel like poet Christina Georgina Rossetti, who long ago asked:

What can I give Him, poor as I am?
If I were a shepherd, I would give Him a lamb.
If I were a wise man, I would do my part;
What can I give Him?
I know. I will give Him my heart.

You can do that this very moment by accepting His Christmas gift to you, eternal life. If that is the desire of your heart, tell Him. While a prayer cannot save you, Jesus can. Allow this prayer to express the desire of your heart:

Dear Lord,

Thank You for coming to Bethlehem and clothing Yourself in flesh . . . for me. Thank You for dying on the cross . . . for me. I receive Your free gift of eternal life by faith right now. Forgive me of my sin. I open the door to my heart to You. Come in today . . . come in to stay. I accept Your free and gracious offer of forgiveness. Thank You, Lord, for the gift of eternal and abundant life and for coming to take up residency in my heart right now.

In Jesus' name, amen.

You have just begun the great adventure for which you were created, to know Christ, whom to know is life, abundant and eternal. Begin to grow now in your newfound faith. You can continue the journey you have started with *The Christmas Code* by beginning January 1 with a daily walk with Him throughout every day of the new year with *The Believer's Code: 365 Devotions to Unlock the Blessings in God's Word.*

About the Author

For more than twenty-five years, O. S. Hawkins served pastorates including the First Baptist Church in Fort Lauderdale, Florida, and the First Baptist Church in Dallas, Texas. A native of Fort Worth, he has three earned degrees (BBA, MDiv, and DMin) as well as several honorary degrees. He is president of GuideStone Financial Resources, which serves 250,000 pastors, church staff members, missionaries, doctors, nurses, university professors, and other workers in various Christian organizations with their retirement and benefit service needs. He is the author of more than thirty books, including the bestselling *The Joshua Code*, *The Jesus Code*, and *The James Code*, and he preaches regularly at conferences, universities, business gatherings, and churches across the nation. He and his wife, Susie, have two married daughters and six grandchildren.

Follow O. S. Hawkins on Twitter @oshawkins.
Visit www.oshawkins.com for free resources.

MISSION:DIGNITY

All the author's royalties and any additional proceeds from the Code series (including *The Christmas Code*) go to the support of Mission:Dignity, a ministry that enables thousands of retired ministers (and in most cases their widows) who are living near the poverty level to live out their days with dignity and security. Many of them spent their ministries in small churches that were unable to provide adequately for their retirement. They also lived in church-owned parsonages and had to vacate them upon their vocational retirement as well. Mission:Dignity tangibly shows these good and godly servants they are not forgotten and will be cared for in their declining years.

All the expenses for this ministry are paid for out of an endowment that has already been raised. Consequently, anyone who gives to Mission:Dignity can be assured that every cent of their gift goes straight to one of these precious saints in need.

Find out more by visiting www.guidestone.org and clicking on the Mission:Dignity icon, or call toll-free at 888-984-8433.

UNLOCK THE BLESSINGS IN

God's Word

Available October 2017

The Believer's Code invites
readers into a 365-day
journey. Adapted from
The Joshua Code, *The Jesus
Code*, *The James Code*, and
The Daniel Code, as well as
brand-new applications and
takeaways for readers, this
first 365-day devotional
from O. S. Hawkins includes
a short devotional reading,
scripture, and a Code Word
for each day, along with a
challenge to put their faith
in practice.
ISBN: 978-0-7180-9953-4

THOMAS NELSON
Since 1798